-E-
~~Fic~~. 743.697   14605
                                                $8.90
             Frame

Drawing The Big Cats

DATE DUE

JA 17 '84			
MR 2 '84			
FE 12 '85			
AG 2 '85			
APR 28 '86			
JUL 8			
MAR 20 '89			
OCT 2 0			
OCT 15 '99			
JAN 31 '00			

Imperial Public Library
Imperial, Texas

DEMCO

DRAWING THE BIG CATS

DRAWING THE BIG CATS

BY PAUL FRAME

A GROLIER COMPANY

A HOW-TO-DRAW BOOK
FRANKLIN WATTS
NEW YORK/LONDON/TORONTO/SYDNEY   1981

Library of Congress Cataloging in Publication Data

Frame, Paul, 1913—
  Drawing the big cats.

  (A How-to-draw book)
  Summary: Discusses tools and techniques of drawing and presents instructions for drawing the tiger, lion, leopard, cheetah, and their cubs.
  1. Lions in art — Juvenile literature. 2. Tigers in art — Juvenile literature. 3. Drawing — Technique — Juvenile literature. 4. Artists' tools — Juvenile literature. [1. Cats in art. 2. Drawing — Technique, 3. Animal painting and illustration] I. Title. II. Series: How-to-draw book.
  NC780.F69   743'.6974428   81-2966
  ISBN 0-531-04321-5   AACR2

Copyright © 1981 by Paul Frame
All rights reserved
Printed in the United States of America
6 5 4 3 2

CONTENTS

Introduction **7**

CHAPTER 1
How to Begin **8**

CHAPTER 2
Exercises **15**

CHAPTER 3
Anatomy and Proportions **19**

CHAPTER 4
Perspective **25**

CHAPTER 5
Putting It All Together **31**

CHAPTER 6
Learning About Light, Shadow, and Tone **41**

CHAPTER 7
Drawing the Tiger, Lion, Leopard, and Cheetah **51**

CHAPTER 8
Drawing the Cubs **59**

CHAPTER 9
Added Tools and Techniques **66**

Summary **72**

INTRODUCTION

Don't ever say you can't draw.

If you can control a pencil enough to write, you can draw.

Expressing yourself with crayon or pencil is something most of us did at a very early age. Your first efforts may have been scribbles, but the more you tried, the more control you gained, and the better the results were.

This came about for a number of reasons. Two of the most important were total concentration and a strong desire to please — both yourself and others.

The same is true now and the only way you can improve whatever you do is by doing it.

Don't think this means that you have only to practice to become perfect. Talent will have much to do with how skillful you become.

Compare your present work with your past work. **Don't compare** your work with that of someone else. **Study,** but **don't compare.**

Draw as often as you can, but draw only as long as you remain interested.

Whatever degree of drawing skill your practice brings to you, very few efforts will give you more excitement and pure pleasure.

CHAPTER 1

How to Begin

As you become more relaxed and sure of yourself, you will want to branch out, to try different materials, to experiment. That's as it should be — but for the present the materials mentioned below will be all you'll need.

Drawing Board: You can buy one at any art supply store; recommended sizes are between 14 to 18 inches (35 to 45 cm) wide by 20 to 24 inches (50 to 60 cm) long. If you want to save money and make your own, here are several suggestions. Use 1/4-inch (.6 cm) plywood, or glue together two or three pieces of thick industrial cardboard or three pieces of corrugated board. Be sure to alternate the ribbing as shown. Cover any of the homemade boards with a piece of linoleum; it makes a good smooth drawing surface.

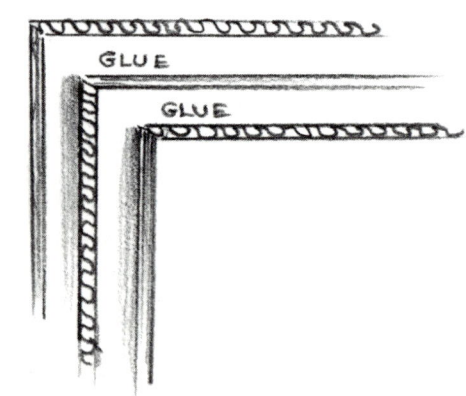

Paper: This can be expensive, so for your exercises and practice sessions use large grocery bags. Slit these down one side and at the bottom.

If they are very wrinkled, dampen and then press with a steam iron.

Another idea is to save newspapers. Then from a paint or art supply store buy a can of liquid gesso. Give each side of each sheet two coats of gesso. Allow fifteen minutes of drying time between coats. This will not cover the print completely but it will cover enough for your practice sessions.

Your local art supply store will have a number of types of sketchbooks and drawing pads in stock. Which one is best for you is something you must decide.

The only advice offered here is **not** to choose a paper that is very smooth or slick or one that is very thin. The exception to this is tracing paper. It will be most useful and will be discussed later.

Pencils: Drawing pencils come in many degrees: 6B (softest) to HB; 9H (hardest) to H. For your first few weeks HB and/or 2B will be most useful. However because your paper absorbs moisture readily, 4B or even 6B will be best for damp days.

If you use a wood-cased pencil, keep a pocket sharpener (A) nearby. Another suggestion is one of the inexpensive automatic pencils (B). The slender leads in HB or 2B make it unnecessary to sharpen frequently, except for very fine detail.

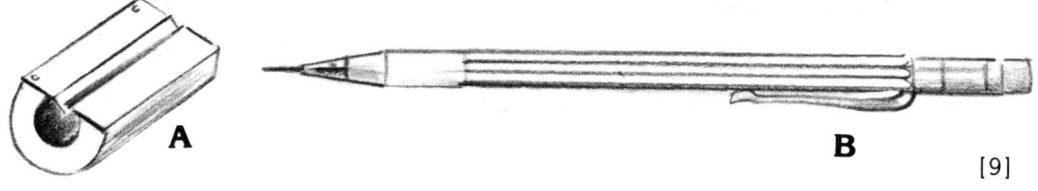

A   B

Another choice could be lead holders (C). Lead for these holders ranges from 8H (very hard) to 6B (very soft). However, these leads are somewhat thicker than the automatic leads so you might find a sandpaper block (D) useful for sharpening. You can make your own and it might save you money in the long run.

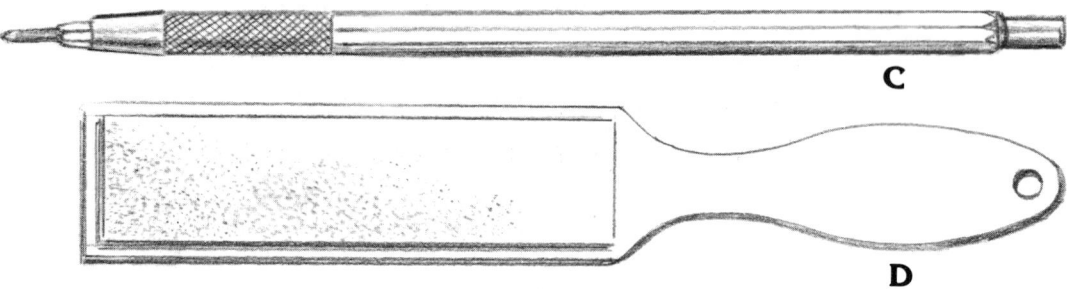

Buy several sheets of 00 sandpaper. Cut these into 1 x 4 inch (3 x 10 cm) strips and staple six or eight to a heavy piece of cardboard (E).

Pencil holders: It is expensive and wasteful to throw away stubby pencils, so a pencil holder (F) for hard-to-hold pencil stubs is an excellent tool to add to your list.

Large clip: A large paper clip such as G is very useful for holding loose drawing paper or your pad to your drawing board. Such clips can be found at most variety or stationery stores.

Erasers: There are three types of erasers that you should know about. The first and most useful is the kneaded eraser (H). It can be squeezed into many shapes and sizes (I) for use in small or oddly shaped areas.

The kneaded eraser is also effective for lightening a line or an area of shading without totally erasing it. DO NOT rub as you would with other kinds of erasers. Place the eraser over the area to be lightened, press, then lift up. Repeat until you have the tonal value you want.

The traditional pink or green rubber, or the more recent plastic, eraser is for removing a line or a tonal value completely.

A note of caution: try to erase as little as possible. Making few mistakes means you MUST think ahead. And that is a particularly good habit to strive for.

The third type is the art gum. This is the best eraser to use if you are working on a glazed or delicate surface.

Fixative: This is a must on your list if you want to preserve your pencil sketches. It comes in a spray can, and all art supply stores carry it. Ask for odorless, workable, matte fixative.

Tracing paper: It comes in pads of three different sizes: 9 x 12 inches (23 x 30 cm), 14 x 17 inches (36 x 43 cm), and 19 x 24 inches (48 x 61 cm).

This kind of paper will be an invaluable tool for you over the next few months. Suggestions for its use will come a bit later on in the book.

Sketchbook: There are many kinds and sizes on the market. Pick one that fits handily into your pocket.

Animals may be your main interest, but sketching anything and everything is the best possible practice. Sketching can only add to your skill and teach you to really **see** and **remember** what you look at.

Instead of a pencil, carry a ball point pen. The ink dries instantly, and therefore there are no smudges. More important, it tends to force you to make simpler and clearer sketches.

Reference file: No matter how good a memory you have, it's unlikely you will remember everything you see. So a file of photos of all the subjects that interest you can be invaluable. It isn't likely you will have models handy for each practice session, so pictures from your file can be most helpful.

Start at once to collect from the magazines and newspapers that are in your home. Add to that supply by asking your friends for theirs. Clip anything that interests you. Divide these clippings into subjects, with each subject in its own folder. To save money, make your own folders. Use either cardboard or corrugated board in strips that measure 17 x 10 inches (43 x 25 cm). Fold 8 inches (20 cm) on each side, leaving 1 inch (2.5 cm) in the middle. Now label each according to content.

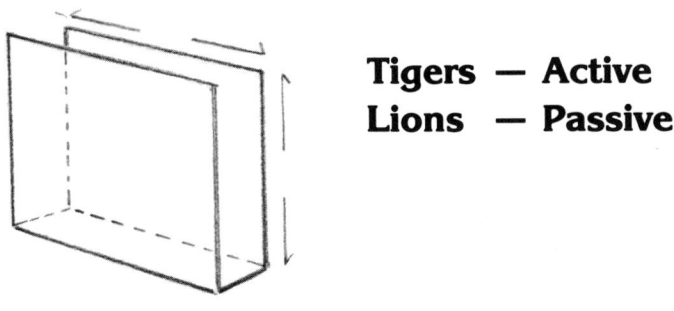

Tigers — Active
Lions — Passive

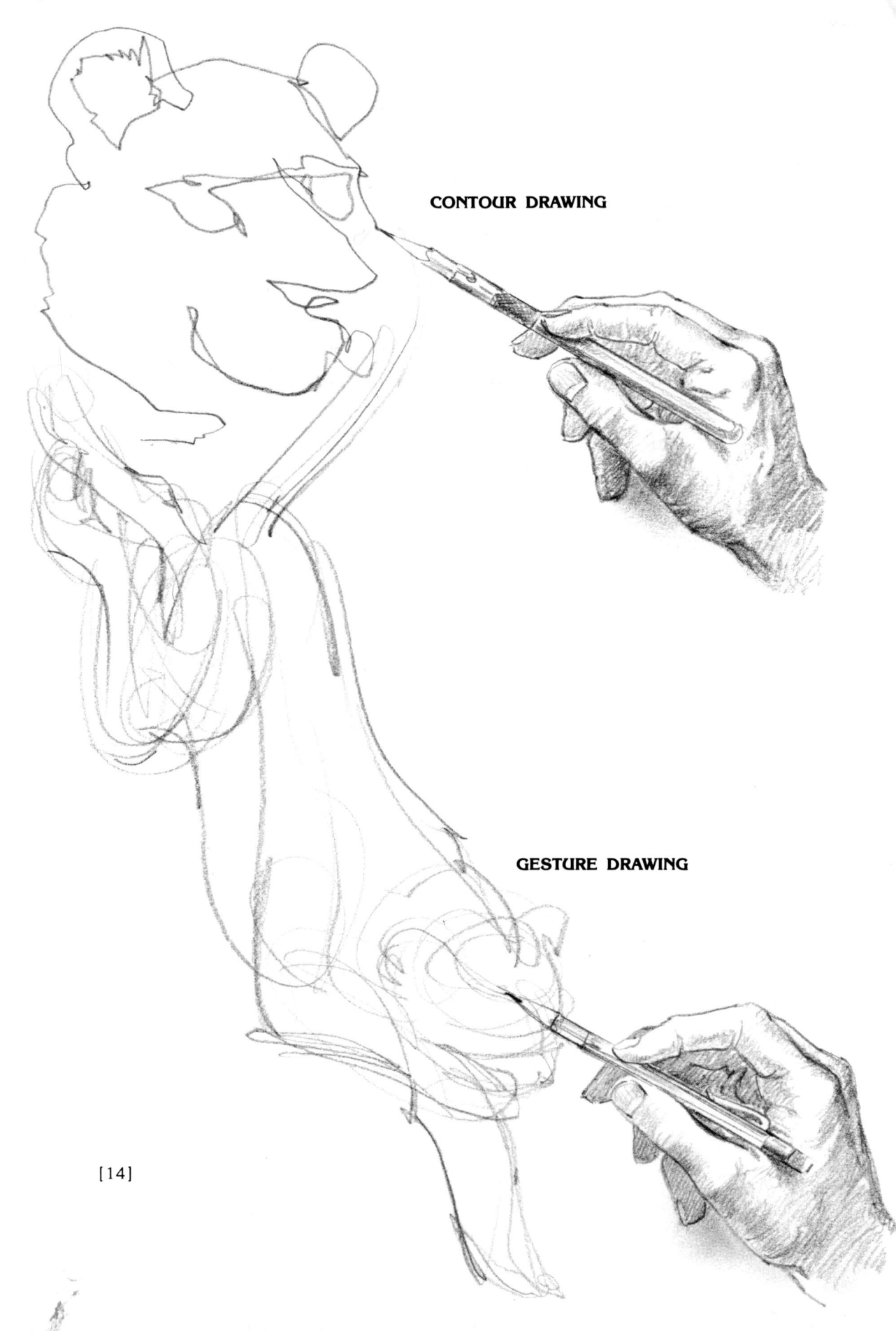

CHAPTER 2
Exercises

Just as members of an orchestra always have a short period of tuning up before they play, you should as well. You are not an orchestra but you are, in a way, a trio. You must tune and coordinate your brain, your eyes, and your hands.

There are two exercises that are top-notch for this. One is called contour drawing, the other gesture drawing.

Try each exercise for about ten minutes. Do them before you start your sketching period.

Contour drawing: Try this one first, using a 2B or 4B pencil on the gesso-coated newspaper, paper bags, or whatever large scrap paper you have.

Choose an object that is simple in form for your first few weeks, perhaps a waste basket, a pitcher, or a vase.

Relax in a comfortable position 6 to 8 feet (1.8 to 2.4 m) from your subject. Pick a starting point along the object's contour. Now place your pencil on the paper and try to imagine that the pencil is physically touching the outline of the object. DO NOT TAKE YOUR EYES AWAY FROM THE OBJECT TO LOOK AT YOUR PAPER.

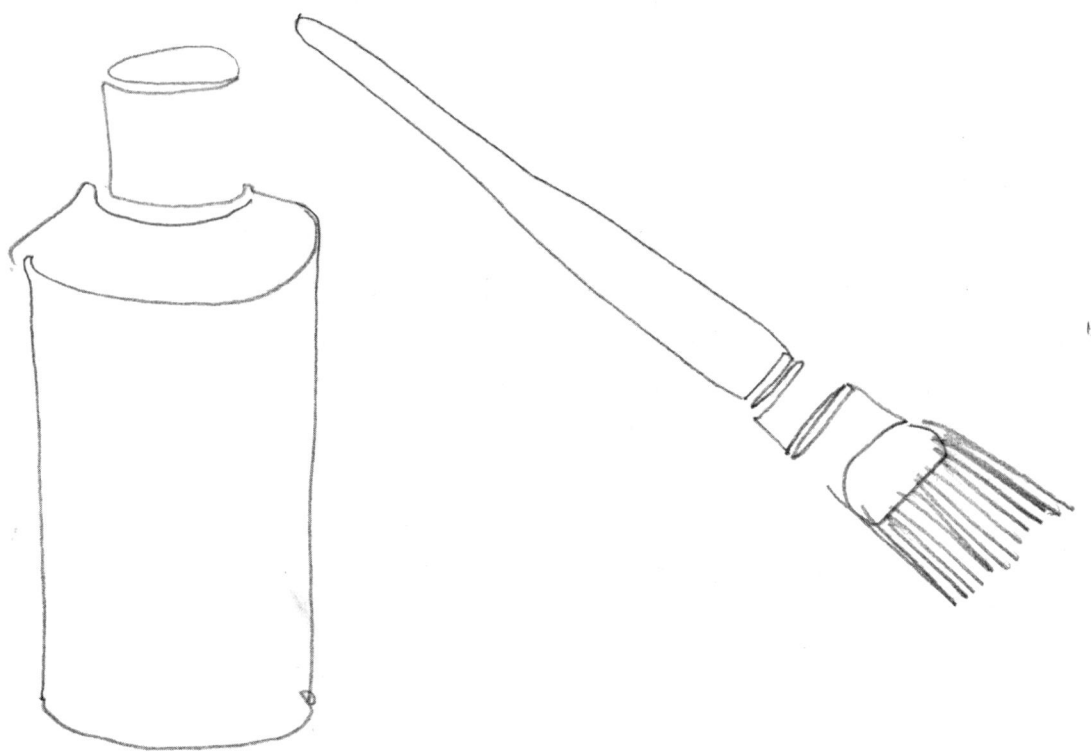

Now very slowly move your eyes and pencil along the contour; move them as though they were one.

This won't be as easy as it sounds. More than once you will be tempted to look at your paper. DON'T! Just move at a very slow pace, observing, trying to "feel" the object. Raise your pencil only when you think you are back to your starting point. If there are details within the object, pick a new starting point and repeat the procedure.

Your first efforts will probably be a panic. Don't be discouraged. Remember that you didn't do very well the first few times you tried roller skating!

Keep all of your exercise drawings for a month and be sure to date them. At the end of this time take them out and you will be amazed.

Gesture drawing: In gesture drawing, you strive to capture a "sense" of what the subject is doing rather than a precise likeness. Don't make a conscious effort to keep correct proportions.

Concern yourself only with showing the feeling of the action or mood. Never mind any of the drawing niceties.

Spend no more than two minutes on each gesture drawing.

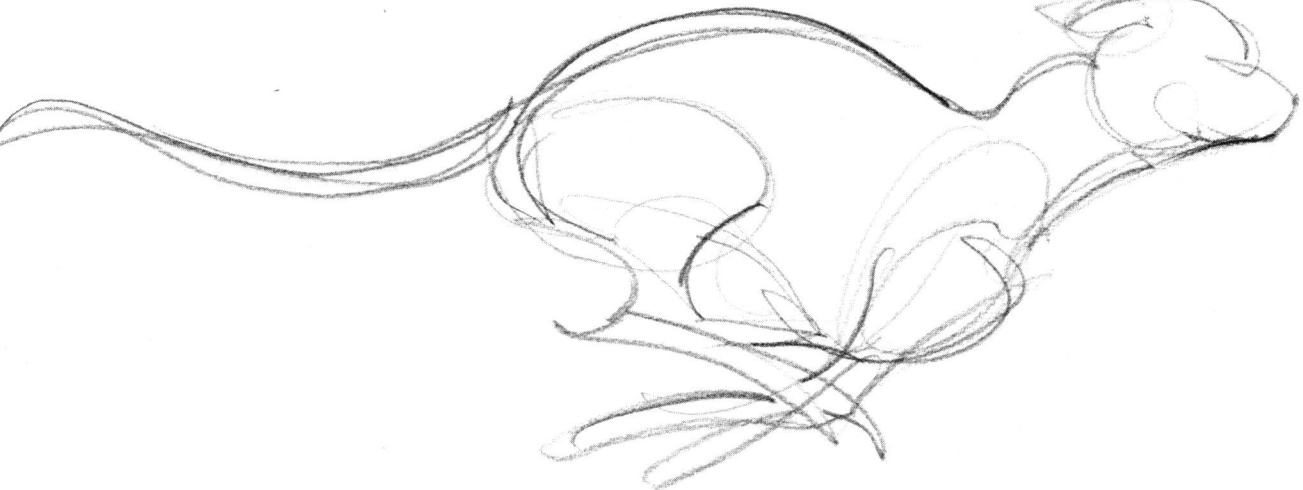

Again, DO NOT LIFT THE PENCIL from the paper. Sketch with as much freedom and abandon as you can. Use long, sweeping strokes; think of your shoulder as the hinge and move your whole arm from there rather than using your wrist. This means using fairly large sheets of paper and lots of them. So perhaps the grocery bags would be a good choice.

Remember to save and date these. A later look will help.

CHAPTER 3

Anatomy and Proportions

The skeletons of a man (A) and a tiger (B), below, are shown in the same position so that you can easily see their differences and also their similarities.

In your new reference file look for a good side view of a tiger, lion, or leopard. Place a sheet of tracing paper over the sketch on this page. Using the sketch as a guide, try to draw the skeleton.

When you have become well acquainted with the anatomy of the big cats, do the same thing, but this time use more difficult views.

This will be a very informative method for you to use until you are totally familiar with the anatomy.

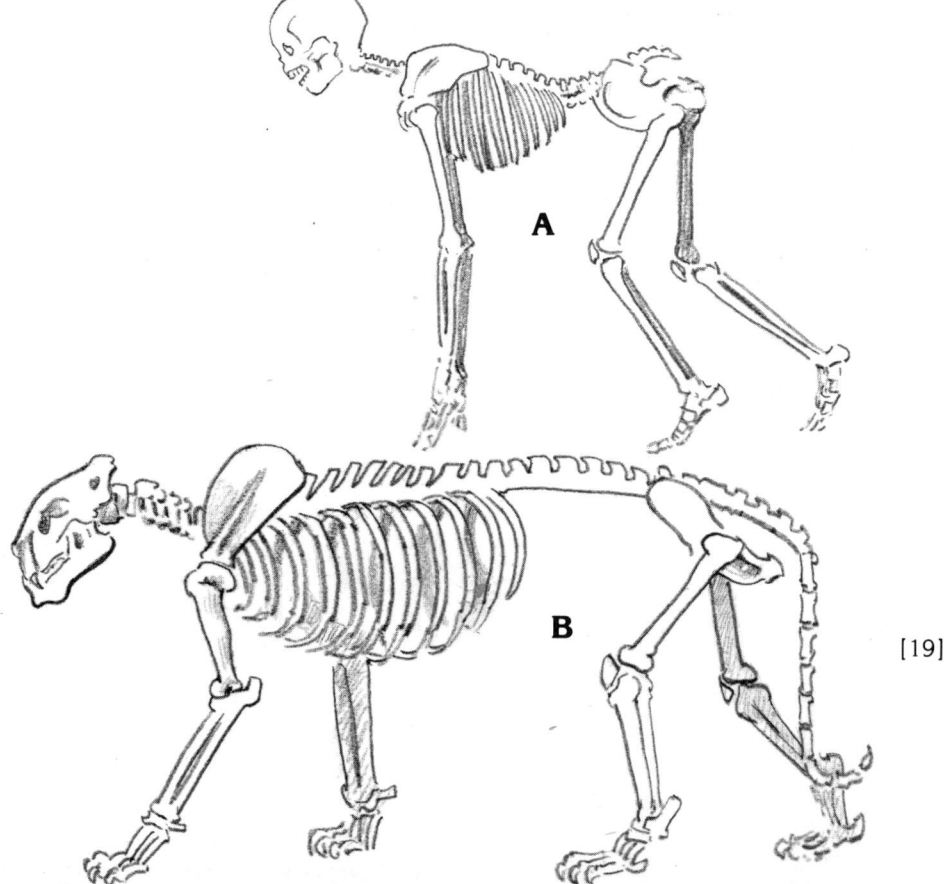

Understanding the skeleton is very important. It is equally important to understand the muscle structure (A).

The muscles that overlay the skeleton create the outward appearance that you see. It is important that you understand the function of both the muscles and the skeleton.

There is a real bonus in learning about both as there is an amazing similarity in the skeletal and muscular structure of all four-legged animals. They may differ in size and development, but the leg, neck, and trunk structures will be in the same general position and they perform the same tasks.

By learning this lesson well you will have a good understanding of most four-legged creatures.

It would be very constructive to continue the use of a tracing paper overlay and draw the muscle structure as you did the skeleton.

For those of you who want more detailed information, there are several good books to seek out. Perhaps the best for you to start with is Charles R. Knight's **Animal Drawing: Anatomy and Action for Artists.**

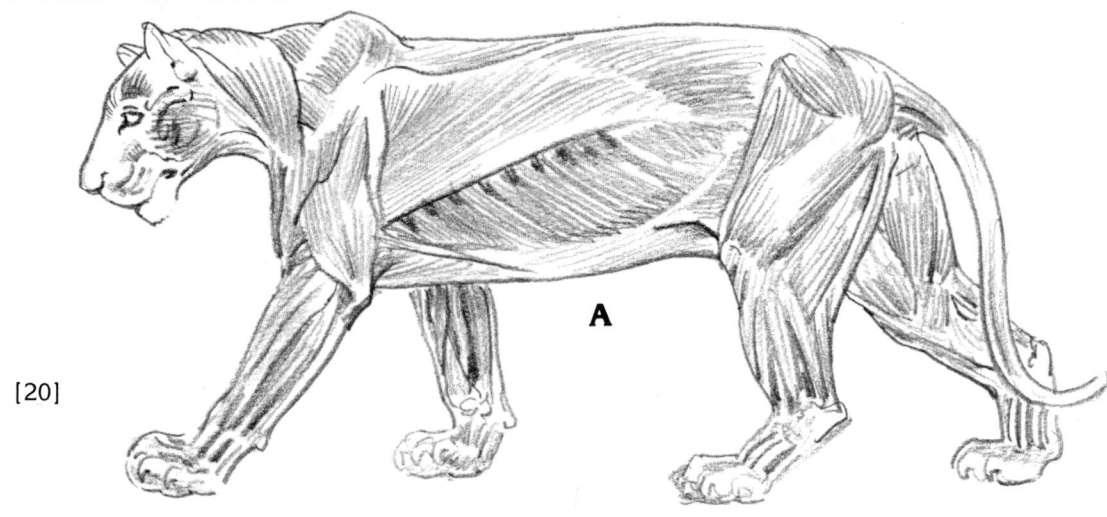
A

There are no hard and fast rules that govern the proportions of animals. They have individual differences just as humans do.

Always remember to check frequently the relationship of one feature to another.

Examples: Are the eyes in the proper relationship to the ears? Have you sketched the tail in proper relationship to the hindquarters?

The trunk (A), from the top of the shoulder to the beginning of the tail, is roughly three times the length of the head in profile.

The legs (B), from the point where they join the trunk, are about one-quarter of the length of the body.

The tail (C), which is an extension of the backbone (or spine), is slightly shorter than the length measured from the trunk to the top of the shoulder to where the tail joins the trunk.

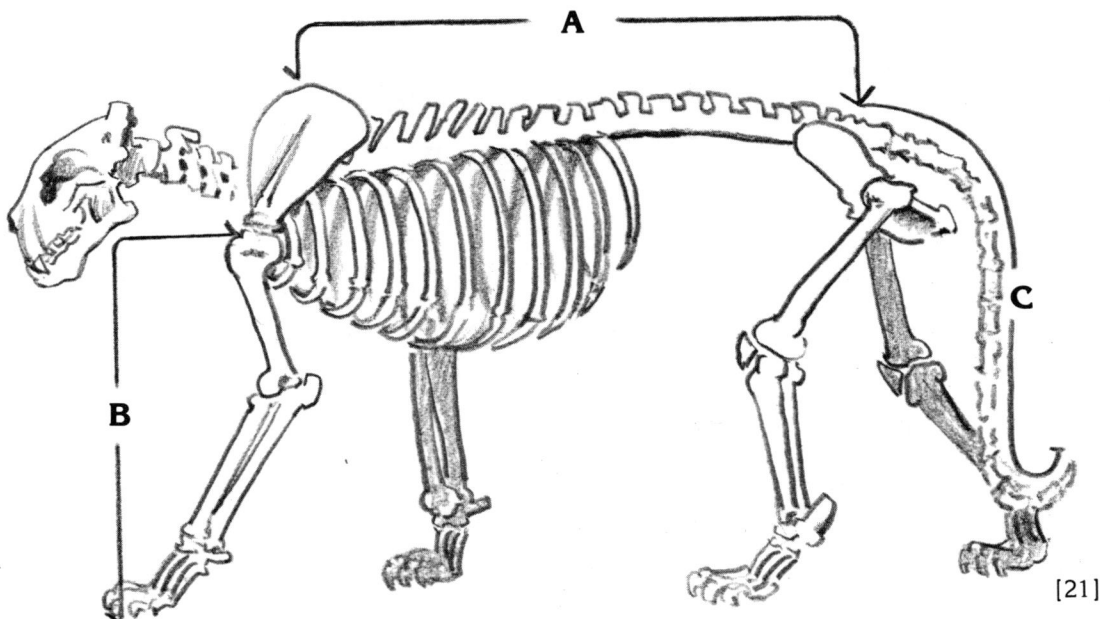

Before you go any further, it would be wise to consider using the following method to rough in your sketches.

This method is called blocking in, and that pretty well says it. Block in your subject first by using large, simple areas.

Consider each area to be a plane, with each plane indicating a change in direction.

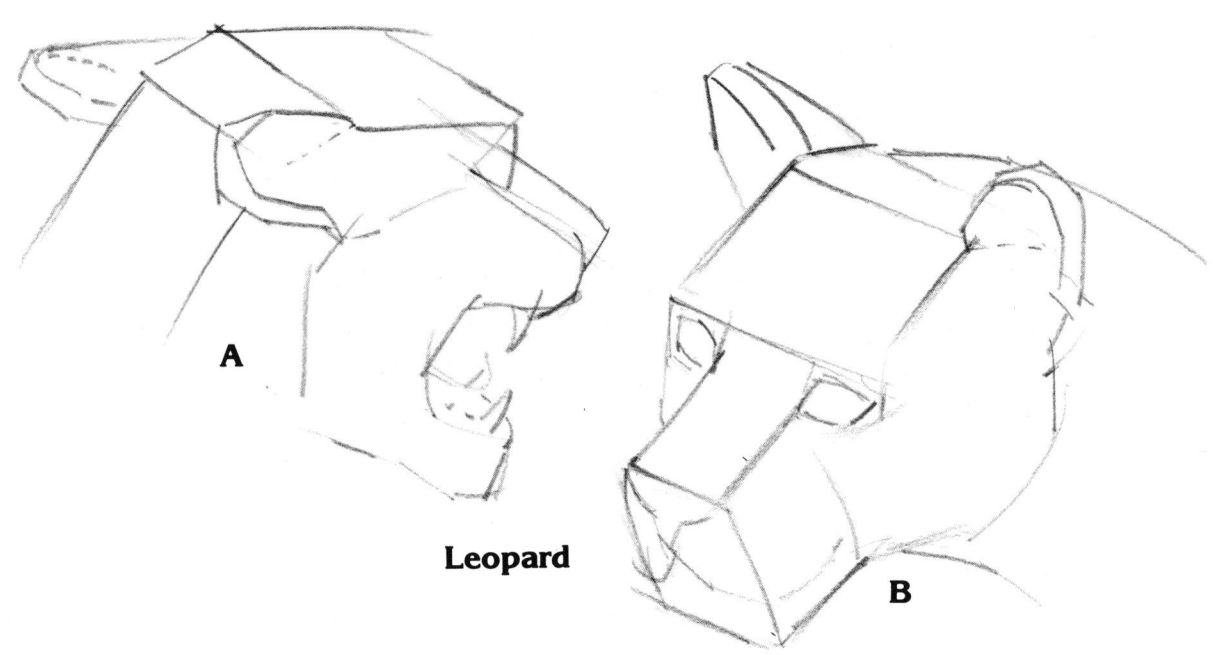

Leopard

When you have finished your blocking in, use the tracing paper as an overlay and begin to refine your rough sketch.

Remember that whenever you draw, you are not just drawing the contour or outline of your subject. You are **enclosing a solid** form. Always try to imagine the unseen side.

From this point the book will deal with the big cats in the flesh. That doesn't mean that you shouldn't keep in close touch with the pages dealing with the skeleton and the muscular structure. Refer to them frequently, at least until you can draw both structures without referring to those pages.

The following are a few hints that will help you in the first few weeks.

In a head-on full view, the distance between the ears (A), the outside of the eyes (B), and the width of the muzzle (C) is about equal. (The muzzle is the width of the jaw.)

In some breeds of the cat family (specifically the cheetah), the muzzle tends to be a bit narrower.

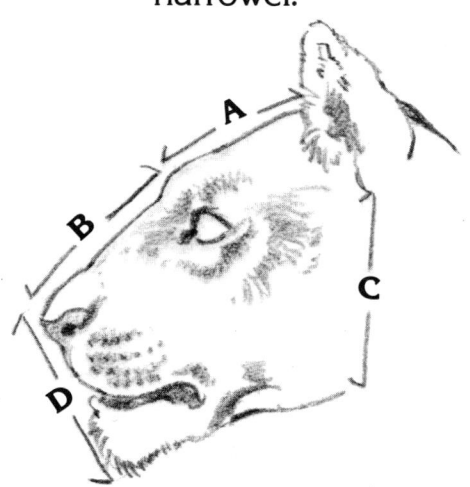

In profile, the distance from the base of the inside of the ear to the end of the brow (A), from the end of the brow to the tip of the nose (B), from the lower base of the ear to the base of the jaw (C), and from the tip of the nose to the bottom of the forepart of the lower jaw (D) is about equal.

This is not always true, but these are guides to help you become accustomed to proportions.

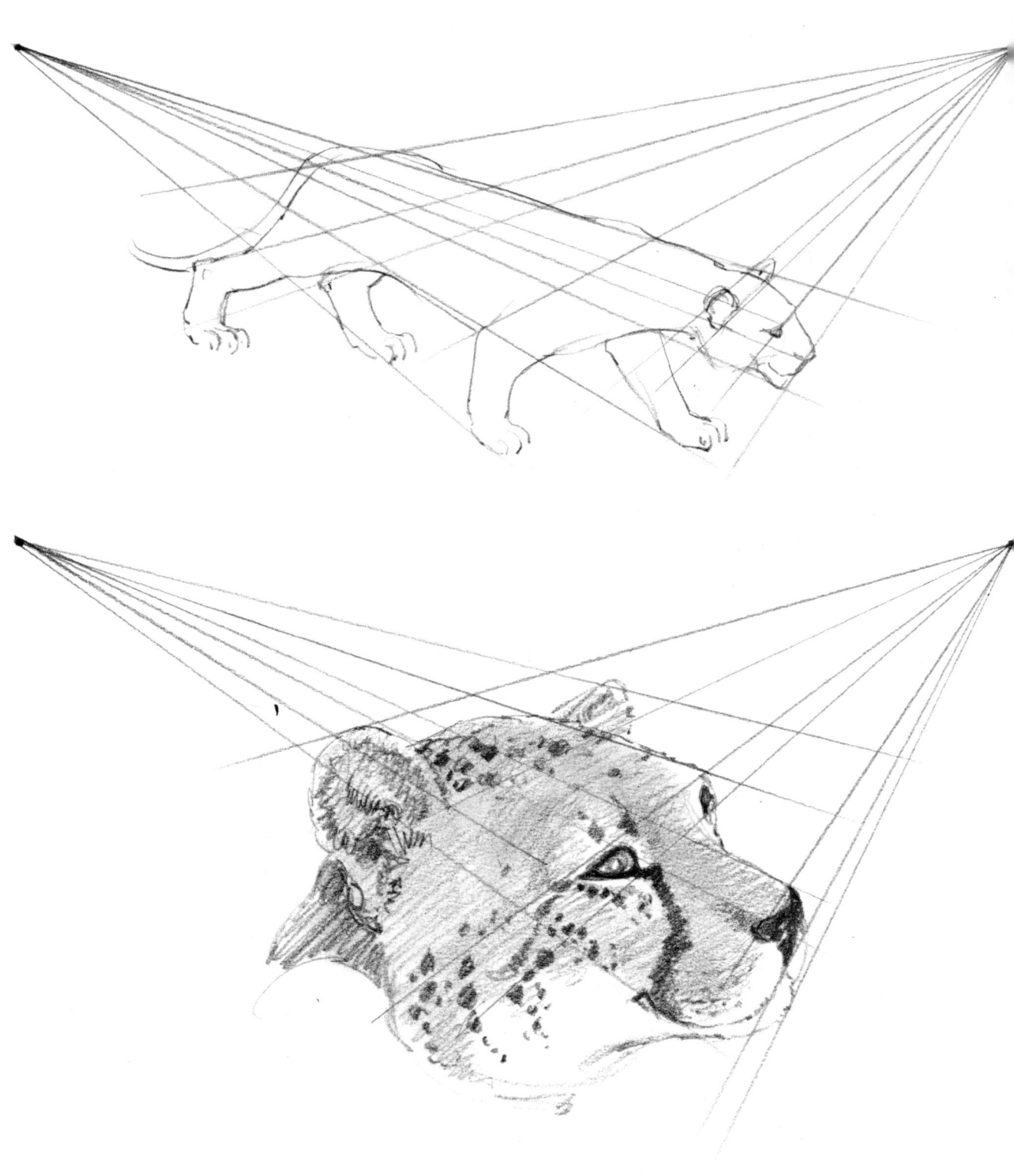

CHAPTER 4

Perspective

Until now you have dealt with proportions and forms as you see them in simple full front view or profile.

Now you face a new challenge. Each time your subject changes position, some part of its anatomy will appear to alter its shape or perhaps even its measurements.

While a movement may cause forms to compress or stretch, they remain basically the same forms. Only the movement has caused them to appear changed.

To draw these changing forms so that they appear natural in any position, not distorted or misshapen, you must understand perspective as well as anatomy.

Perspective is the method used to create the illusion that an object on a flat surface has form and depth.

A knowledge of perspective will be indispensable to you, and you will use it almost every time you draw. Many times, however, your use of it will be so subtle you will be unaware of it.

The next five pages will deal with a simple explanation, and the exercises shown are important.

Try each in turn until you feel you completely understand the process.

A simple cube will be used as an example to help you understand perspective and its use.

The two main tools of perspective are vanishing points (VP) and station points (SP).

The station point (SP) is where you are or imagine yourself to be when you view your subject.

The vanishing point or points (VP) are what you establish to help you to draw your subject accurately and create the illusion of depth.

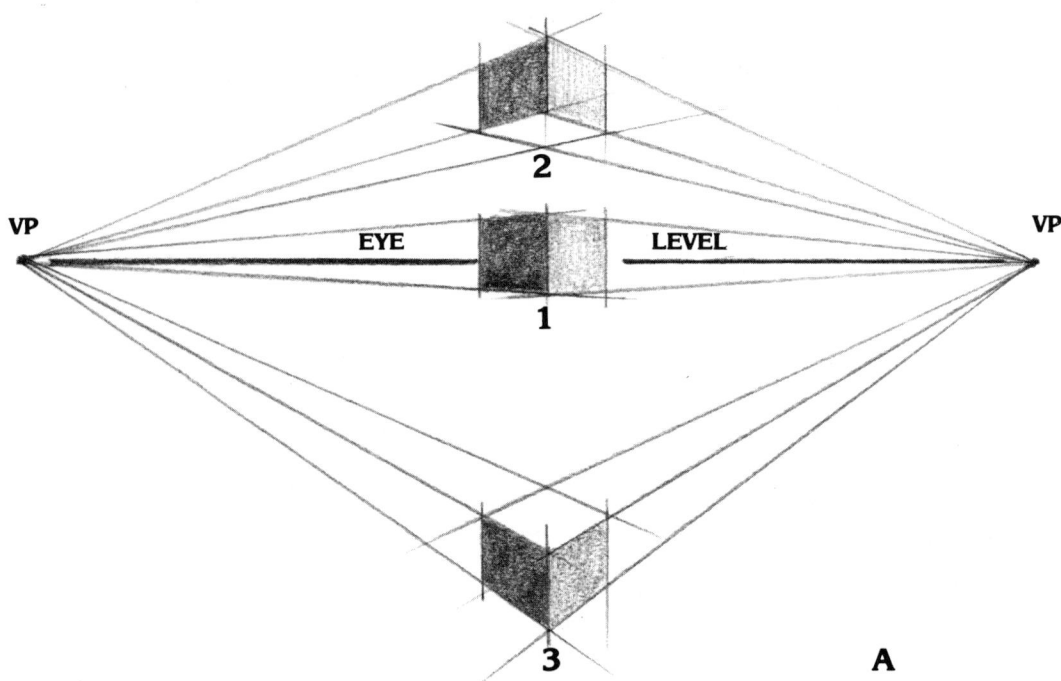

The position of your VPs can be flexible. However, a good beginning rule is to measure three times the width of your object, then place a VP left and right at eye level (Figure A).

Eye level is the point at which, looking straight ahead, your eyes observe an object.

There will be times when only one VP will be needed to check your drawing. One of these is when you are sketching and only showing two planes (Figure A).

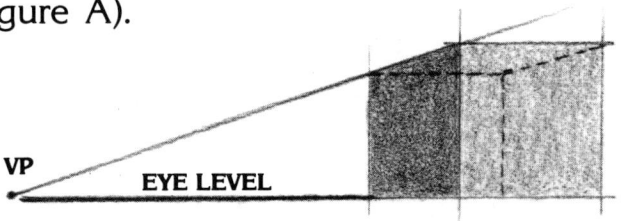

In Figure B, two VPs are used because you are showing three sides or planes of your subject. You are looking below eye level.

If you wanted to show your subject from below or looking up at it, turn this book upside down. You will then be looking up at plane 1.

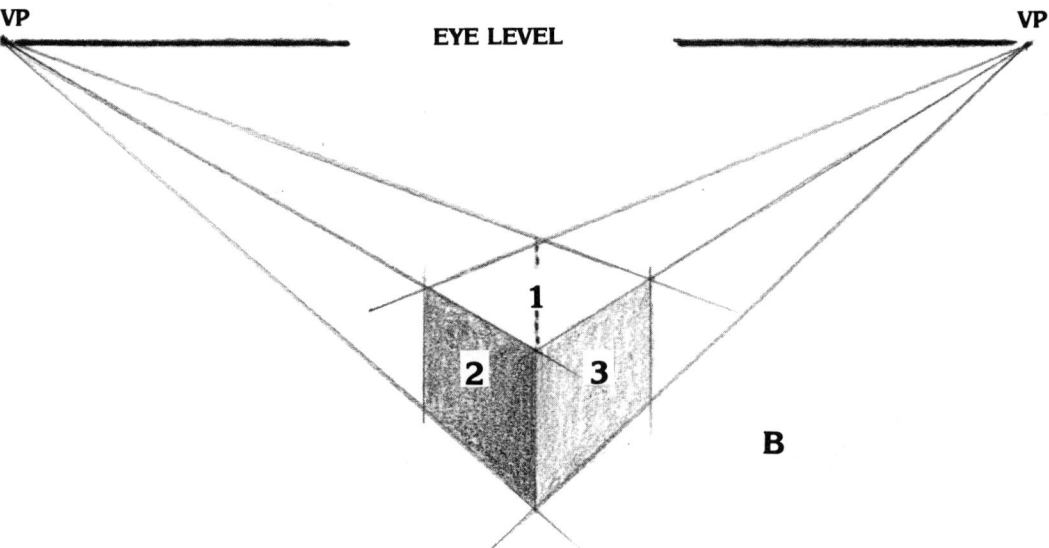

You will notice that because the VPs are relatively close to the cube, the cube seems a bit distorted. The further away the VP, the less distortion there is.

It has probably occurred to you to ask what all these cubes have to do with learning how to draw lions, tigers, leopards, or cheetahs.

While the following might seem a bit forced to you, let's take the examples from page 27 and use them as a basis for two sketches. You should see how VPs can give you a constant check on how accurate you are.

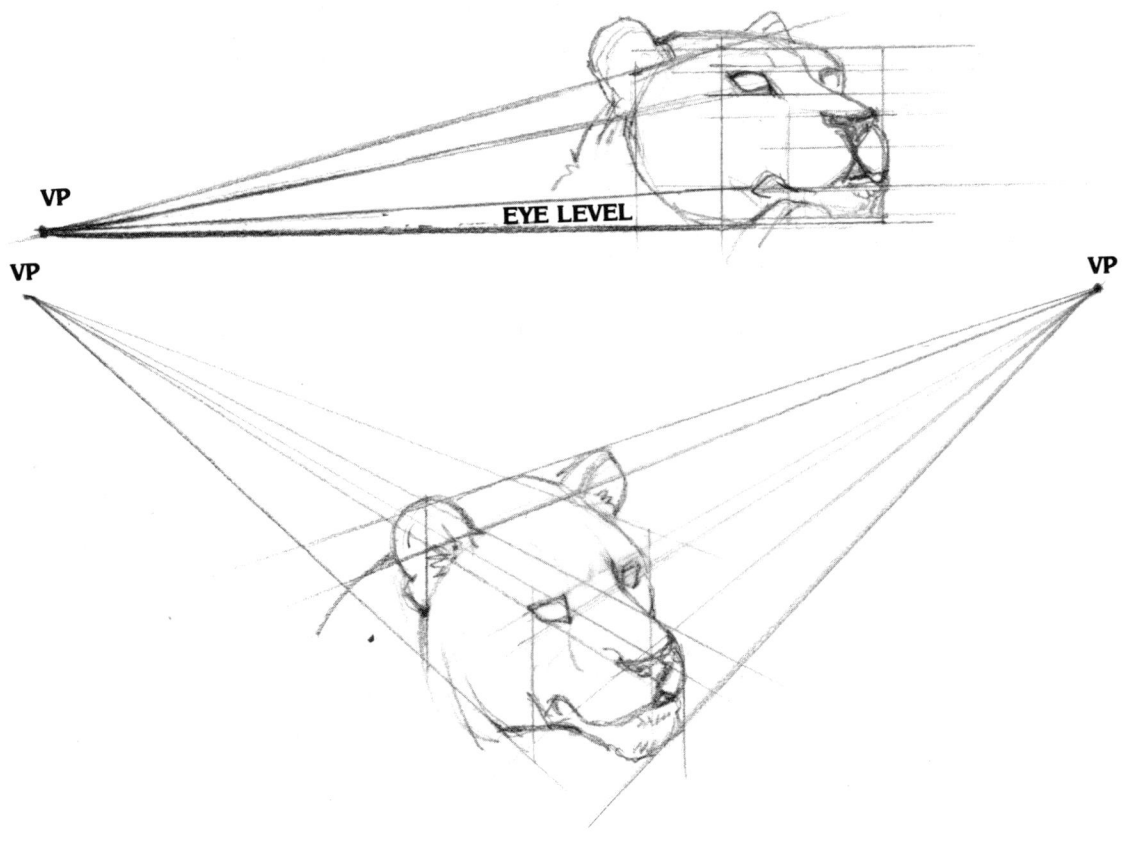

For the next few weeks it would be a good plan to sketch, then check the VPs with a tissue overlay.

Here, in quick review, are the facts for you to remember and practice every time you sketch.

Figure A is seemingly a simple, flat rectangle. Yet by using a VP you can turn that rectangle into an object with form (Figure B).

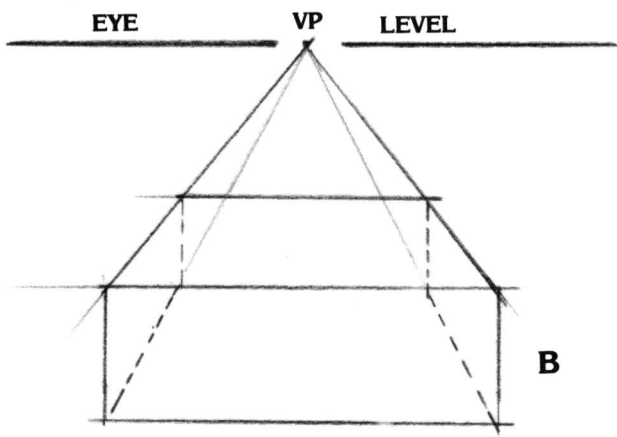

Now we can give added solidity and form by using a second VP. See Figure C.

In each case the dotted line has been used to make you conscious of the unseen forms. This awareness of the unseen forms must become second nature to you if your drawings are to have a solid look.

CHAPTER 5

Putting It All Together

By now, if you've worked through to this point step by step, you are ready to take on the demanding and exciting task of drawing one of the big cats as a whole animal.

The most important guidelines to keep in mind are:

What you are drawing is a dimensional form: it has planes you cannot see. But your drawing must make you feel what you cannot see.

For this reason it is suggested that you add a kind of see-through drawing (see next page) for a few weeks. Do this until you feel your sketches have a good sense of solid form.

Continue with the blocking in as well.

You should think of your particular interest, the big cats, as having four main parts:

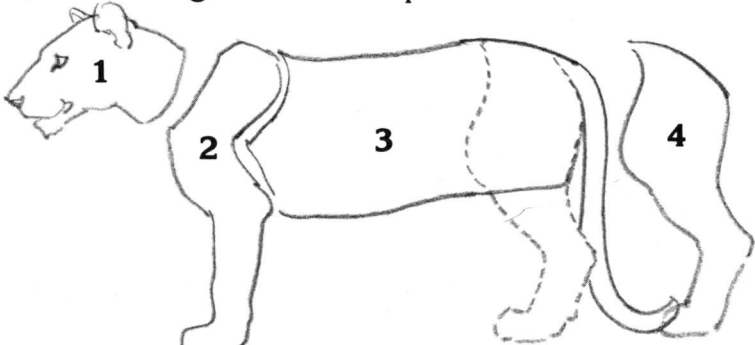

(1) The head and neck, (2) the forelegs, (3) the trunk, and (4) the hindquarters.

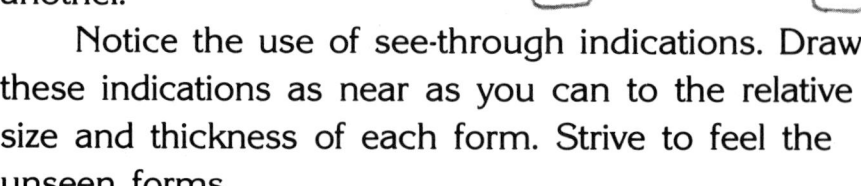

Begin using this simple profile view to put the pieces together in their proper relationship to one another.

Notice the use of see-through indications. Draw these indications as near as you can to the relative size and thickness of each form. Strive to feel the unseen forms.

Figures A and B below illustrate a very important point in drawing any of the four-legged animals. The animal's trunk is suspended between the legs as in A, not sitting on top as in B.

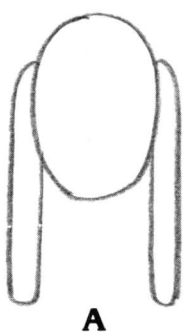
A

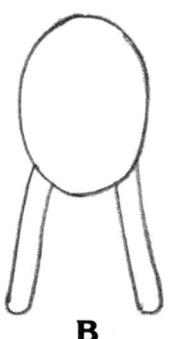
B

For the next few pages we will explore the big cats in more or less passive positions.

The emphasis will be on anatomy and the relationship of one part to another.

Use the following pages as a guide to your next stage of learning to draw.

Here the main problem is to keep the tiger's trunk from looking like something more than a lump.

This means you must work on the anatomy and understand why each form looks as it does. Having trouble? Take a piece of tracing paper and see if you can draw the skeleton.

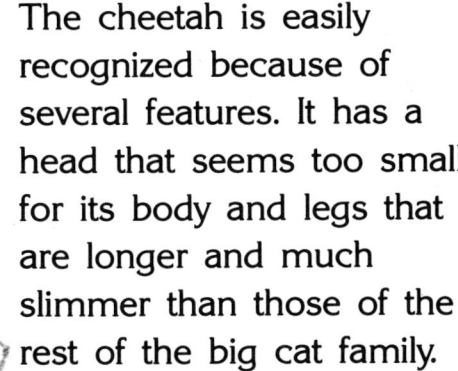

The cheetah is easily recognized because of several features. It has a head that seems too small for its body and legs that are longer and much slimmer than those of the rest of the big cat family.

Here you must strive to make the cheetah seem to be seated firmly on the ground—more easily said than done.

The difficulty here is in the definition of the hindquarters. Notice that the leopard is between the tiger and the cheetah in size.

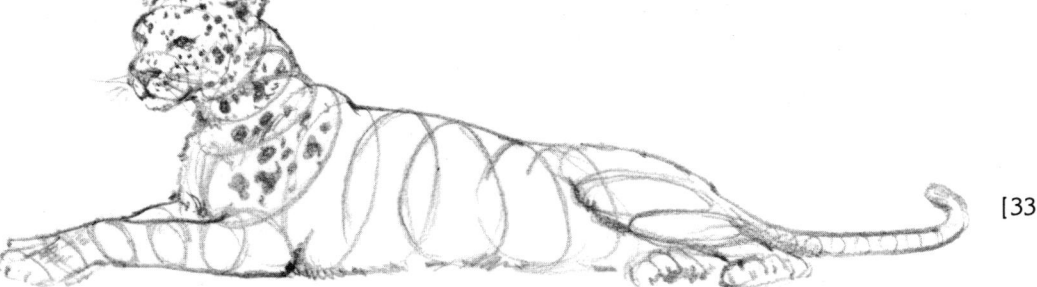

Compare this lioness with the sketch of the cheetah on page 33.

While they are in about the same position, notice how different they appear physically.

Being able to capture these different characteristics quickly in each breed is very important.

Go over each of the four main parts and list, in your mind, how they differ from each other.

Compare the two back views and sketch both to help fix in your memory the differences.

The entire trunk of the cheetah is more streamlined and less powerful. It is much like the difference between a racing car and a well-built pickup truck.

The lioness's head is heavier and much larger. The brow of the cheetah is more rounded.

Pages 33, 34, and 35 should prove a most useful point.

What is basically the same position can be changed, at times almost dramatically, simply by changing your point of view.

Perhaps that seems a simple fact—and an obvious one—but nothing could make a stronger argument for knowing the anatomy of your subject.

Because you know and understand the anatomy, you immediately understand the changed appearance.

Therefore you can draw it much more easily and with authority.

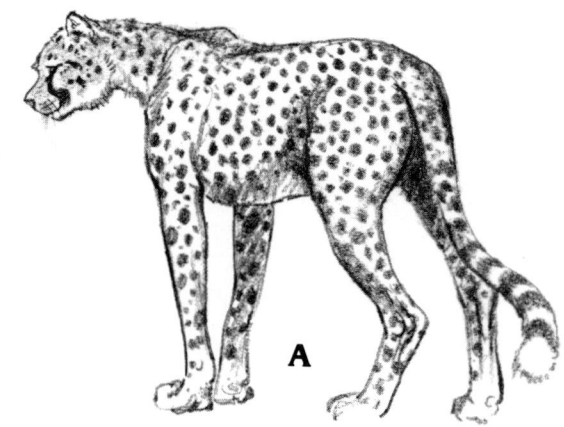

This cheetah (A) and the lioness (B) and the lion (C) are part of a continuing effort to make you familiar from all points of view with these magnificent cats.

There is a tendency for beginners to concentrate on one or two successful points of view. If you want to become a good artist, you must be able at some point in your development to sketch these animals without any reference or model.

    That may be some time in the future, but it must be one of your goals.

Practice, using these sketches. First block in and then refine your sketch with a tissue overlay. If any part or parts of your sketch don't look right, work with a tissue overlay and check the anatomy.

The next step along the way is to work on the animal in motion.

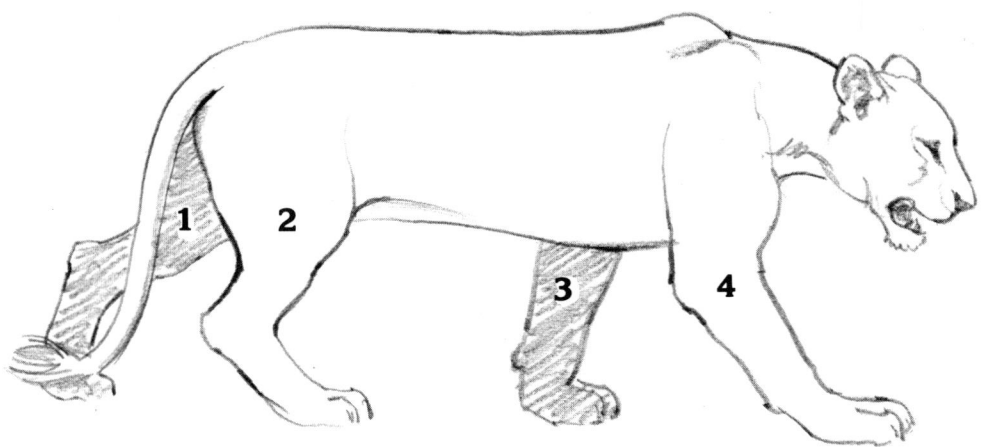

Legs 1 and 3 work together and move to the rear. Legs 2 and 4 move forward. The weight is more or less evenly distributed.

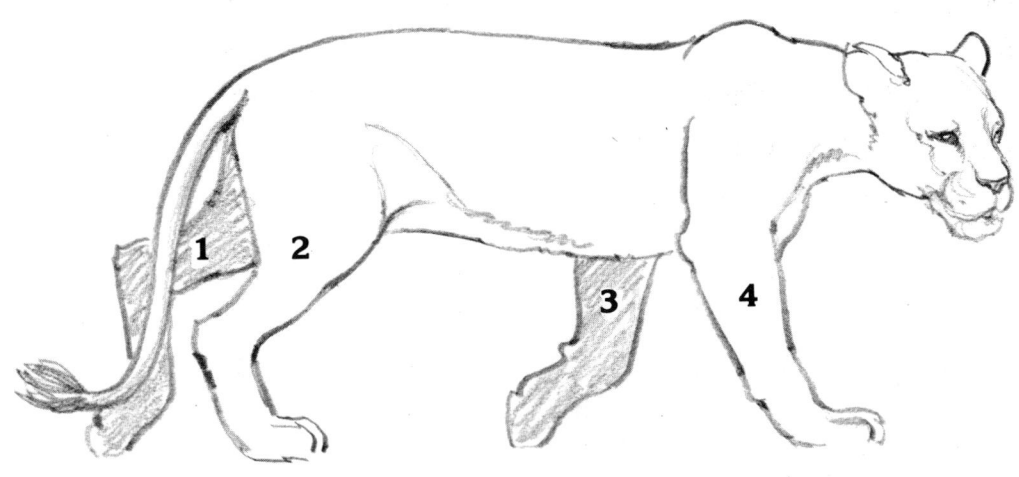

Legs 1 and 3 have moved all the way back and are off the ground for the move forward. As you see, the weight is now carried by 2 and 4 only.

During the walking gait you know that 1 and 3 work together and that 2 and 4 work together.

Unlike their cousins, the house cats, big cats usually carry their tails and heads lowered.

The cheetah is the real "race horse" of the cat world. Below are sketches of three stages of the gallop for you to work from.

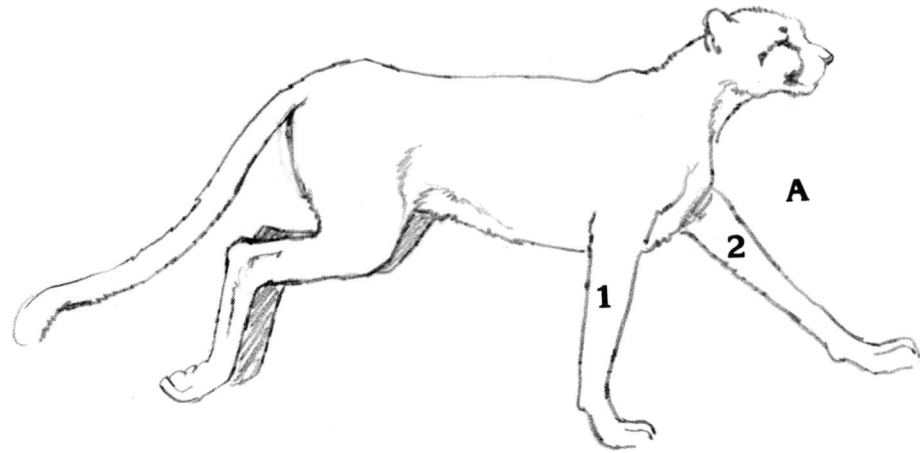

Figure A. For this instant the cheetah's full weight is on foreleg 1, to be followed at once by foreleg 2.

Figure B. Then both hind legs at once take over and give the power for the next stride.

Figure C. Here is the moment when all four paws are off the ground and are best described by the phrase "flat out."

There are many points to keep in your memory. You might burn out a memory cell if you tried to remember everything at once!

Keep the following uppermost, and the rest will fall in place in time. It will help to use this book to review these points every so often.

1. Work out a schedule and really try to stick to it.

Here is a suggestion for a schedule that you might find helpful:
- Try to have at least three one-hour sessions a week.
- Start with ten minutes of contour drawing, then ten minutes of the gesture exercise.
- Follow this with forty minutes of anatomy and sketching.

2. Get to know your anatomy. It is your passport to sound drawing.

3. Continue to block in until you can quickly do a well-proportioned sketch.

4. Always think "in the round." Be conscious of the unseen forms.

5. Constantly check the relationship of one form to another. It will help a great deal to keep your proportions correct.

6. Do not be discouraged if you have a dry spell when you don't draw well. It happens to us all.

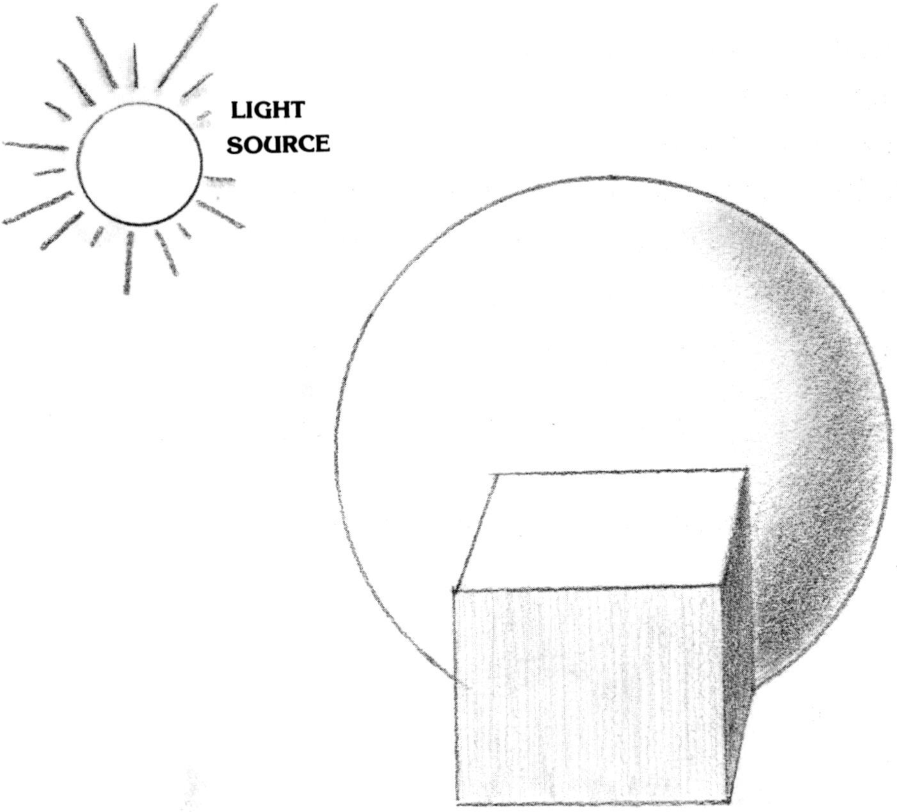

LIGHT SOURCE

[40]

CHAPTER 6

Learning About Light, Shadow, and Tone

Light, shadow, and tone are three exciting words. When you understand them a bit better, they will add a new and rich dimension to your drawings.

This book will give you only the basic facts. A fuller understanding will require you to search on your own—from other books and with lots of observation.

To begin with, you need only know of light, shadow, and the three main tonal values.

Full light: any area unshielded from the source of light.

Shadow: any area shielded or partially shielded from the source of light.

These two simple forms help to make those statements clear.

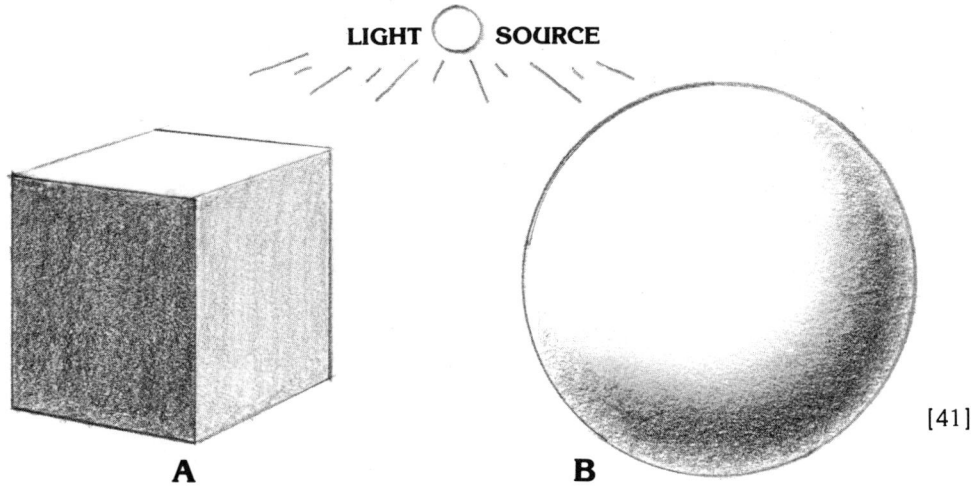

A   B

Armed with those two simple facts about light and shadow, you can—by using good sense and careful observation—visualize how light affects simple forms.

Most big cats are observed under outdoor lighting conditions. Therefore outdoor lighting should be first on your list.

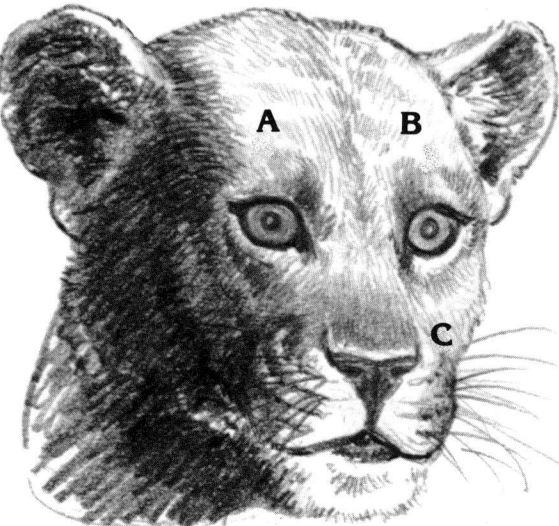

This head is very simplified, with a few secondary shadows shown. These are caused by bone formations of the eye sockets (A) and (B), and the light side of the muzzle (C).

The most important characteristic of this shadow is its soft edge. This is caused by the light hitting rounded forms (example B, page 41).

Hold an egg up to a strong source of light. Now hold any small box or cube up to the same light. Do you see how much softer the edge is on the egg's shadow?

Your increasing knowledge of anatomy and constant sharp observation will lead you to see, then understand.

Tone: a term that describes the values used to shade your drawing surface—from white to gray to black.

Until you are ready to go beyond this book, NEVER use more than three tones.

1 **2** **3**

1. A pale tone, about 10 percent of the darkest value of your 2B or 4B pencil.

2. A medium gray, or about 50 percent of your darkest value.

3. As dark as your 2B or 4B will mark. Establish this tone first. It will quickly tell you if others are needed.

Never use three tones if two will do, or two if one is enough.

In applying tone, your pencil strokes should always follow the direction in which the hair grows.

In areas where the change is slight or confused—such as the inside of the ears—blend your strokes so that they don't show direction.

Mr. Ears, three months old, is a good example. Study a house cat, where the growth is the same.

Block in the head of this lioness and then proceed with the other suggested steps. A lioness was chosen because she has no distinctive markings to complicate your first efforts at light, shadow, and tone.

Remember to keep your "blocking in" lines quite light so that when you start the refining process the lines you erase won't continue to show.

The quality of line you use in your refining should be as suggested here, as continuous and clean as possible.

Avoid a worked-over, scraggly line such as this:

At this stage you can strengthen any weak spots in your drawing. Then carefully begin to indicate, with **very** light line, the areas where you are going to put tone.

Consider that your light source is coming from the upper right-hand corner.

Don't get too involved — keep the shadow areas simple. Remember to establish your darkest tone first. It becomes far easier that way to keep your other tone or tones in place.

If by now your drawing begins to look too worked over, or has had too many erasures, start a new one.

This lion's head takes just a shade more of your newfound knowledge. The head is held a bit higher, so you will be required to use your perspective.

Using the same four steps as shown on pages 44 and 45, try using this head as guide.

To give a little added zest to the problem, this time make your sketch one-third larger than the first one. Below is how to scale it up.

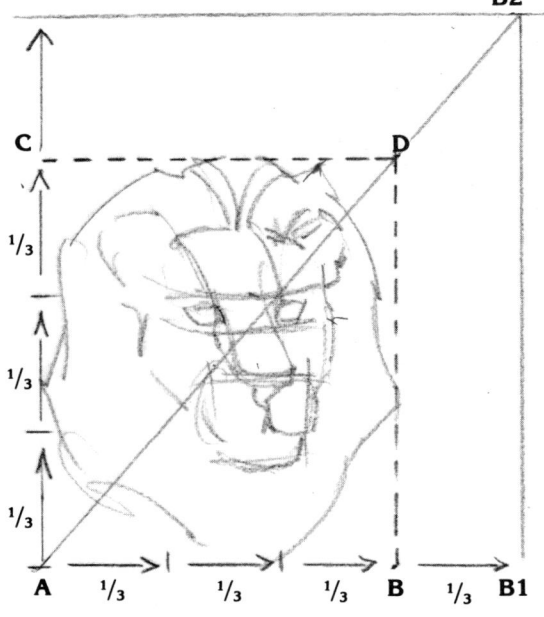

Determine the height and width of the lion's head (points A to B and A to C). Run a very faint line from C straight across, one up from B (dotted lines). Where they meet completes the outer dimensions of your picture. Now add one-third to your width (B1). Run a faint line straight up (B1 to B2), and then a faint line from A to D where it bisects B2. You've got it!

This is the point where you begin to plan where your shadows are to be placed. Remember that your light source is above and to the right of your subject.

The one rule to remember here is that the point at which a form is blocked from or recedes from the light source is when it begins to fall into shadow.

Logic will tell you that the right side of the lion's head, under his lower jaw and inside his ears, is the most obvious place for shadow.

The next few pages will show you how to work on the whole animal.

These two sketches are of a tiger. But, just so you won't have any distractions, he will be a tiger without stripes.

Keep the same light source, above and from the right.

Even though you are dealing with shadows covering a larger area and may feel tempted to try more complicated tonal values, resist. That time will come.

After you have worked on these two sketches for a while, you might try using the sketches on pages 34, 35, 36, or 38. Imagine light sources from different directions. It's good practice and interesting.

As you will naturally be limited in your sources for models, the closest you can come to a live one is your cat or a friend's.

Except for size and weight, the house cat is very close in structure to its larger cousins.

There is also your growing reference file of photographs, and of course if you are lucky, there may be a zoo nearby.

In any case keep the following ready in your mental file.

1. Train yourself to make notes, mental or on paper, of whatever you see. This requires real concentration; most of us cannot remember in detail what we saw yesterday.

It would be great if you would get in the habit of carrying a sketchbook. The notes or sketches you make will be enormously helpful to you later.

2. Establish your darkest tone first.

3. Remember that your pencil strokes should follow the direction of the hair growth.

4. Until you feel at home with the use of light, shadow, and tone, keep tones simple. Cover small areas—just enough to add solidity to your sketch.

CHAPTER 7

Drawing the Tiger, Lion, Leopard, and Cheetah

There are about a dozen species of big cats. They come in many sizes beginning with the tiger, the largest.

Surprised? Most people are. It is usual, when the question is asked, "Which is the largest of the cats?" to answer, "The lion, of course, the king of beasts." This is probably because of his majestic appearance and because of the fact that he is certainly the loudest of the cats.

So it is the tiger first, then the lion, followed closely by the jaguar, the leopard, and the cougar, sometimes better known as the mountain lion or puma.

Next is the fastest known animal in the world, the cheetah.

The rest of the dozen or so are big only when compared to the domestic cat.

Largest among the smaller big cats are the serval, the ocelot, and the lynx. These are very closely followed in size and weight by a variety of cousins such as the margay and the caracal.

We will deal with most of the truly big ones, the tiger, lion, leopard, cougar, and cheetah, mainly because these are the ones you are most likely to see live in zoos or to know through pictorial research.

Resident of Asia and largest of the cats, a fully grown male tiger can weigh up to 600 pounds (272 kg) and measure up to 11 feet (3.4 m) from the tip of his nose to the end of his tail.

Aggressive, but at the same time careful, hunters, tigers are usually loners. Although they prefer a forested terrain, they are sometimes found in both open and mountainous areas.

Because relatively little is known about the mating habits of tigers in the wild, experts are not sure if they mate for life. It is known that a mother and cubs for up to the first two years of the cubs' lives do form family groups. Then they drift apart to seek their own areas. The female may have from one to four cubs in each litter.

The lion fears nothing and has only one natural enemy, man. Among its own kind it is good-natured, playful, sometimes quite noisy, and above all lazy. The male may spend up to seventeen hours a day sleeping or resting.

The females do most of the hunting, sometimes in teams. Yet the male eats first and best.

Lions are the most social of the cats, living in groups, called prides, of as many as thirty. The pride is ruled by one dominant male. His rule is that of a benevolent despot; all goes smoothly if the "king" isn't challenged.

The leopard, whose average weight is about 140 to 150 pounds (64 to 68 kg), is considered by many the toughest of all the big cats. It is also the meanest, most aggressive of the lot and a real loner. The male spends little time with his mate and almost never sees his cubs.

A shrewd and patient hunter, the leopard is also the only one of the cats that will kill more than it can eat. It seems to enjoy killing game.

The leopard is at home in all kinds of terrain in Africa and parts of southern Asia.

One of the fastest known animals, the cheetah has been clocked at 70 miles (113 km) per hour for a distance of 300 yards (274 m). Beyond that distance, cheetahs tire rapidly.

Everything about the cheetah is designed for speed, including an extra-slow heartbeat.

Cheetahs are mild-natured, even a bit timid, and have a birdlike chirrup instead of a roar or growl.

The mother, minus the male, heads a family group. The cubs remain in the group until they are two years old and then they go their separate ways.

This most elegant of the cat family has the added distinction of nonretractable claws.

Cougars, or mountain lions, as most people are inclined to call them, are from 6 to 8 feet (1.8 to 2.4 m) long from tip of nose to end of tail.

By nature they are not very aggressive except when extremely hungry or when the female's cubs are threatened.

The cougar is native to both North and South America and has been seen from Hudson Bay to Cape Horn.

Perhaps its best known characteristic is its cry or scream. At night the sound has weakened the knees of many a hunter.

Its favorite method of attack is to pounce from above onto its victim's back.

As you have no doubt guessed by now, this book has assumed that you are seriously interested in drawing, particularly animals. So it is important to sum up this chapter with some good advice.

1. Observe closely and get as many different views of each animal as possible.

2. Get as close to the real thing as you can. It is best, of course, to visit and make sketches at a zoo whenever possible.

3. To test your observation and memory, try making sketches later at home, either from memory or from notes.

4. If at all possible, take photographs to add to your file.

5. See if your library has a copy of **Animals in Motion** by Edward Muybridge, or possibly buy your own.

One of the best ways to help yourself begin to draw with authority is to know as much about your subject as possible. Learn everything you can about all animals. The more you know, the less likely you are ever to draw an animal doing anything false or out of character.

CHAPTER 8

Drawing the Cubs

There is little hope that it would ever be possible for you to work from life. However, there are a few points that will prove helpful in learning to draw the young.

The pups, cubs, or kittens of any animal, when they are under eight weeks old, have a roundness, a slightly "boneless" look. There are no sharp, hard forms, and there is little muscular development.

To do a really good sketch or drawing of a very young animal may prove harder at first than sketching the adult.

By now you have realized that learning any new skill isn't exactly easy. But just look how long it took you to learn to run without falling down. Learning to draw well, to add another way with which to express yourself, will be a life-long satisfaction.

And with drawing, you can't skin your knees when you "fall down."

It is time to stretch your pencil and try your hand at putting two animals together. What better as your subject than mother and daughter?

This is a three-month-old in a quiet moment, of which there are not many at this age. As yet the cub has not begun to develop the long nose characteristic of the tiger and still has the soft, round look so typical of all young animals.

The most interesting thing about both of these sketches is how often the stripes help to define the forms. In both cases, be careful when drawing the foreshortened trunk.

As there can be no favoritism on these pages, here are father and son. Lions make quite devoted and patient fathers in the wild. They've often been observed playing with any number of cubs of the pride.

This is another exercise in perspective, and it probably won't be easy. If it becomes too difficult, move on and return another time.

The great hunter below also presents several problems in perspective. It is a problem you can't practice too often.

These three cougar kittens are about three and a half months old; you will again have to call on your new knowledge of perspective.

Try also to give a plump look to their trunks.

You will notice an attempt to give a furry look by using an irregular line in some places. Try this but don't overdo it; here and there is enough. The effect is gained by using the side rather than just the point of the lead.

By now you should be trying such "adventures." Just don't let them get to be too important.

Cougar kittens are, like African lion cubs, spotted for the first few months.

Here is a cheetah "sandwich" for you. These cubs are about three months old and have just lost a rather long-haired coat that is topped by a pale silver-blue mantle.

Your most difficult problem with this trio will be to keep each one distinct yet very much a part of this three-in-one group.

It might be better for your first try to draw each one as though you could see through the other. Then with tracing paper over that, draw them as you see them here.

With this leopard family you have a chance to work on a number of problems in one sketch.

You will be telling a story, so in a way you can look on it as your first illustration assignment. It might be fun to work on a story leading up to this action.

You will be tackling the job of adding atmosphere to a composition. And it certainly will test your knowledge of anatomy.

There are light, shadow, and tone throughout. Determine your light source.

You are dealing with the motion of a mature animal and cubs. It is a tall order, so don't hurry.

Think about each step.

CHAPTER 9

Added Tools And Techniques

Improving your drawing skills should be your first consideration for some time to come.

However, using familiar tools in new ways and learning to use new tools can add much to your experience and growth as an artist.

These next five pages will make some suggestions as to tools and how to use them. The rest is up to you. Remember, the sky's the limit!

A note of caution: never let your tools or a specific technique become more important than the drawing.

You should always be able to look at a good drawing and have your first thought be, "What a good drawing!" It should never be, "What a lovely rendering! What splendid technique! Nice drawing, too."

With this in mind let us discuss a few facts, beginning with several ways to hold a pencil. Until you find something that works better, continue to use HB, 2B, or 4B (according to the dampness) or a lead holder or automatic pencil with those leads. When you become a bit more sure of yourself, a good old ball point pen will do.

There are four ways to hold a pencil, but only two of these allow you to hold it in a relaxed way and still have full, fluid control.

First is the way most of us learn when we begin to write (Figure A).

The second is to hold the pencil between thumb and first two fingers but **under** the palm (Figure B). This position allows you to use both the point and the broad side of the lead as well.

Both allow the maximum use of your wrist and specific control.

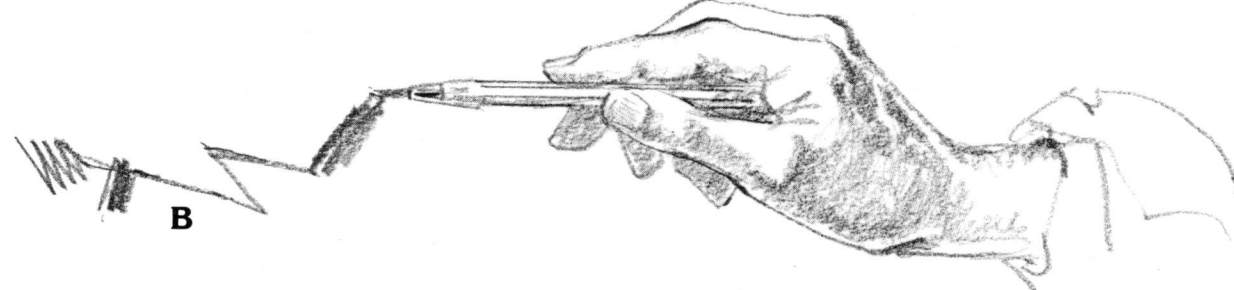

Try them both. One position may allow you to get a certain effect more easily than the other.

There are several kinds of pencils not mentioned in the front of the book that might interest you.

There is the charcoal pencil which comes in a compressed stick as well, in varying degrees of softness.

A reminder here: it is best to spray fixative on all drawings if you want to keep them from smudging.

Another pencil that interests many young artists is the lithograph pencil. You should try all these pencils whenever possible.

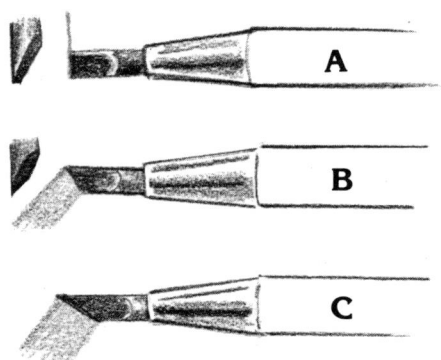

You can sharpen them all — including the compressed stick — as you would a pencil. Or you can make a chisel point (A). This gives you a broad or thin line, depending on how you hold it.

You can make the chisel point a wedge (B). The degree of wedge determines the width of the line (C).

You can make a thin line by turning your pencil so only the thin edge touches the paper.

The compressed sticks are very versatile. You can cover a large area with tone by using the flat side or make a thin line by using one of the edges. If you're not using the flat side, wrap part of the stick with a facial tissue (D). It keeps your hands cleaner.

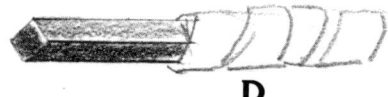

D

Pen and ink is an exciting medium but it is not as flexible as pencil and, of course, your mistakes are harder to change.

Remember to hold the pen as you would a pencil — relaxed.

The pen requires a harder, somewhat smoother surface than a pencil, unless you are using a ball point or regular fountain pen.

For practice sessions you can use bond typewriter paper. And vellum tracing paper is great for pen and ink work. Search out the surface you feel most comfortable working on.

Experimenting is the answer to finding the best pen nib and holder. For a start try Gillot #290 or Hunt's finest. They are both flexible enough to make both fine and broad strokes.

Here are some suggested strokes:

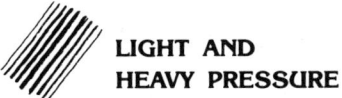 LIGHT AND HEAVY PRESSURE

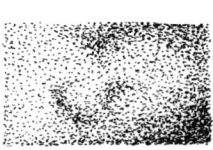 A DOT TECHNIQUE THAT GOES FROM LIGHT TO DARK BY INCREASING PRESSURE

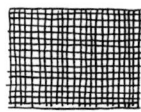  TWO TYPES OF TWO-LINE CROSS HATCHING

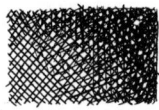 AN EXAMPLE OF THREE OR MORE DIRECTIONS TO BUILD TONAL VALUES

 SHORT, QUICK STROKES, WITH INCREASED PRESSURE TO GIVE TONAL DEPTH

The brush is perhaps the most versatile of all tools. It also requires more practice and discipline in order to do it well.

By using brush and ink you can make a line drawing. By using lampblack and water you can render a black and white painting, **plus** tones of gray.

Buy a pointed #2 or #4 red sable brush and a tube of lampblack. The brush will be fairly expensive, but a cheap one is a bad investment. They simply do not last.

You can, with practice, make all of the strokes suggested for the pen. Practice before you start a rendering.

There are two ways of using a brush. One is to keep it fairly wet. The other is to keep it quite dry.

Put a small amount of lampblack in a dish. Have two glasses of water at hand, one to rinse your brush each time you change the tone and one to dilute a small amount of lampblack to get the tone you plan to use.

Dip your brush into the tone, then, pressing gently, draw it across a blotter until it looks like this:

 **DRY BRUSH**

Now begin to build your tonal values, turning your brush to the narrow edge when you need a fine line.

SKETCH A

DRY BRUSH

SKETCH B

WET BOARD

You will find that you will have to refill, then wipe, your brush a good many times before you get what you want.

Naturally, for the darker areas you will increase the amount of lampblack you use.

In sketch B you will have to work on water color paper. It comes in pads of various sizes, and all art stores have a good selection. Get the least expensive until you feel sure of yourself.

Make your pencil sketch, keeping the line light. Now with a sponge, dampen the area you are going to start in.

As soon as your paper becomes too dry, dampen lightly with the sponge.

Warning: both techniques are difficult to control, so don't get upset if it takes considerable practice to begin to control the medium. But it's a ball!

SUMMARY

In drawing — as in almost everything we do — the foundation is the single most important step.

So on occasion, if you feel impatient and long to cut out all the step-by-step study of anatomy and perspective, go ahead. Spend some time doing exactly as you would like to do. But never draw when you are distracted.

Save the results. Put them away and then in a week or two look at them and decide for yourself how important a good foundation is.

Do not become discouraged. We learn and mature at different speeds. Never compare yourself with another. If you want to know how you are progressing, take out some drawings you did several months ago and that should answer your doubts.

Always keep an open mind and eye toward trying new methods, new tools, and different ways of looking at your subject.